THE PRELUDE GIRL

poems

Marjorie Gavan

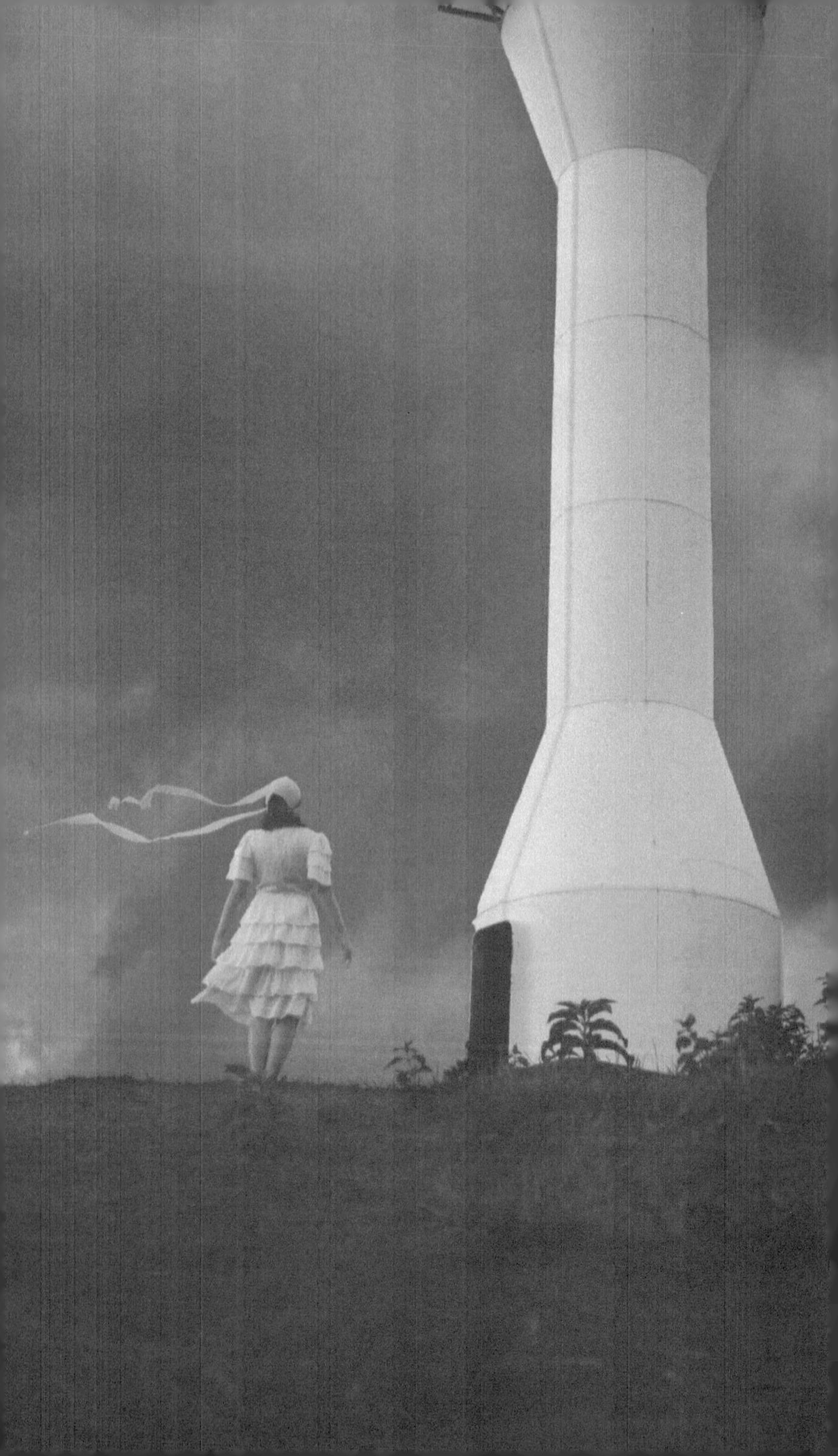

The Prelude Girl

poems

Marjorie Gavan

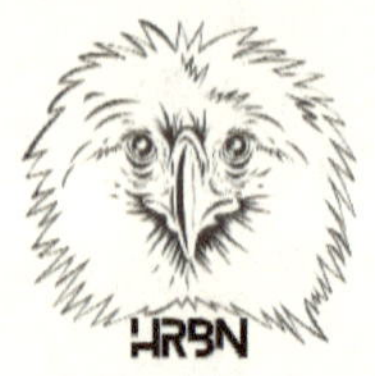

First edition, 2025.

ISBN: 979-8-9918679-2-4.

Cover design: Pains of Disfigurement by Mike Alegado.

Interior layout by Al Christopher Mendoza and Marjorie Gavan.

For more information, contact haribon@haribonpublishing.com or visit the website www.haribonpublishing.com.

Published by HRBN (Haribon) Publishing.

For my brother, Charles.

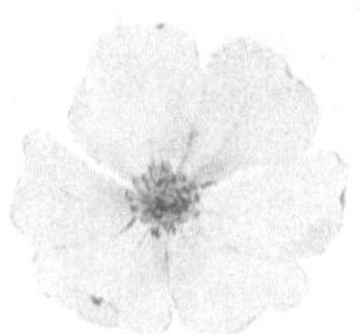

Contents

Preface

My story isn't rare. You've probably heard it before: people who were treated as placeholders, dated just before the real one comes along. The sorrow and rage that come after being abandoned while still burdened with unfinished emotions were all too real.

I never thought I would ever feel that way, and I didn't know how else to deal with the pain, or how to hide my suffering, other than to write poetry.

What name is there for a woman like me? Not quite a lover, not quite a mistake. A fling? A rebound?

One day, the word came to me: **prelude**. **An introduction before the main act**.

I was a **prelude girl**, the person you're with before "the one."

Some of you may think that my poems are too raw and bitter. Some might suspect I haven't moved on (for the record, I have). However, this story needed to be told, not to reopen wounds, but to acknowledge that stories like this happen.

Make no mistake—this is not about him.

This is about people like us, those who were abandoned, sat with the wreckage, and walked out stronger than we've ever been.

This collection is an ode to anyone left with full hearts and nowhere to place them.

I hope through this book, you're able to see your light. Choose yourself, even when no one else does. Especially then.

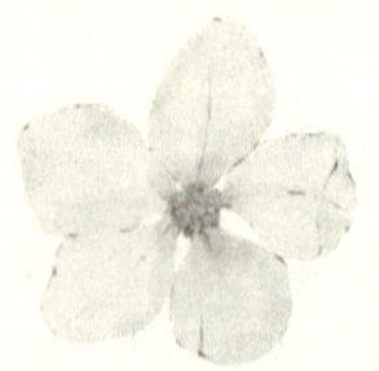

I Am Not Your Comfort

I'd like to warn you,
you didn't come to the right place
if for you the right place is steady.
Like a stroll on level ground,
or the comfort of warm hands on your back.

This, my dear, is a wasteland.
A roost for vultures,
where you're hunted for sport
and devoured mid-breath.

Each door you enter
leads to your most wretched nightmare,
where your scream is smothered
by the dolorous wailing
of all the women who came before you.

Then you'll spend an eternity
reliving your penalty,

obliged to face the horrors you made.
And you will not be able
to turn away.

This place was never meant for you.
Yet it's been waiting.
And I hate to break it to you,
you cannot leave.

You will have to sit through it,
witnessing what you buried.
There is no exit, only a seat,
and a long, merciless watch
As the most vile fragments
of you crawl out
and name themselves.

Dish

That night was bittersweet,
but unreasonably long.
We occupied a table at Dish,
too close to the stage,
where my friends sat,
eyes glazed over,
like a cult making a religion
out of this beautiful man,
who sang as though
he wrote the song
just for you.

The cold seeped through
my black linen top.
I breathed warmth
into my freezing hands.
All the sushi was gone,
but the used chopsticks
lay scattered across the table

as if waiting
to be useful again.

I made a pilgrimage to the washroom
like a devotee,
more times than I could count,
as the liquor thinned my restraint
and deepened my melancholy.
I staggered through the dark,
whimpering in the shadows,
while beautiful people walked past
unbothered,
as cold as the air.

I wanted so much to be seen
that I returned to the table
with a fiction,
to incite the rage
and the concern of my companions.
And just as I began

to revel in their attention,
the room was swallowed by darkness
and the silence made a choir
out of us all.

As this unfolded,
the man began to sing
of a love he had lost.
We locked eyes,
and for one splendid moment,
I was the girl
he had lost.

The Pilgrim

We sat face to face.
You heard my thoughts
for the first time,
brazen, as I held your gaze.
Neither of us knew
we were crossing a line.

Night rolled in.
I remember counting
the hats hanging on the wall.
You turned that room
into a museum of your ego.

And there I was,
pitiful, a willing audience,
hanging on your every word,
hankering for more,
like a devoted disciple.

When you asked me to stay
beyond what was allowed,
I mistook your eagerness,
your hunger for warmth,
as romance.

Where in the room
did you find your cue?
Which word
gave you the courage?
Were you the one seduced,
or was I the one baited?

I wondered,
how many of us
wait in your shadows?
Which of your phones
was I saved under?

Still, I let you in,
granted you permission
to see all of me.
Yet you kept your passion
as if it were a crime.

Years passed.
And I found myself
on the grassy lawn,
staring at your old room,
half-lost behind the trees.

It stood still,
a time capsule
waiting to be exhumed—
to unveil my original sin.

Astral

Our lips were unsuited,
his tongue a trespass
in my droughted mouth,
parched by my inappropriate
years of longing
for his tenderness.

He cradled my cheeks like prey,
searching for my appetite.
My eyes stayed open
long enough to see
this wasn't faithful
to the movies.

It wasn't expected,
yet I let it unfold,
realizing I was susceptible
to his corruption.
That my morals were either

as thin as twigs
or figments of my imagination.

The descent was almost lovely,
as I let him take liberty
all over my skin,
a silent offering,
free from liability.
While he danced through his want,
I slowly rose from my body,
hovering, watching;
more an intruder,
less than a participant.

And the cruelest thing?
After all of it,
he spoke a woman's name,
and it wasn't mine.

Rapids

Let's take our chances in the rapids.
We may survive in one piece.
But should we end up with broken bones,
at least we would know
the consequences of our feelings.

So meet me at the cliff,
And I promise you, my dear,
it will all be worth it.
Don't leave me waiting.

Diplomat

I walked through the halls,
my footsteps echoing in the silence,
checking every room,
peering into the ruins,
imagining how everything looked
in its zenith.
Long before I was born,
I wondered what memories
were still clinging to the walls,
what horrors were hiding in the cracks.

He followed me, wordlessly,
his strides, light as a cat.
But his sighs were as loud
as the clacking of my heels
on concrete
I closed my fist,
wishing that I was afraid of ghosts,
instead of his stillness.

Then I heard him say,

“Why aren’t you scared of these halls?”

I turned to him and said,

"Darling, my mind is a much darker place

than these walls."

My Almost Greatest Love

I didn't fancy him in the beginning.
But isn't that how some love story begins
subtle, unimpressive,
then suddenly necessary?

He was no one,
until he was someone.
Brandishing a guitar,
with a devilish smirk,
carrying an old heartbreak
that made him sound human.

He made himself small for me;
said I was too good,
out of his league.
Said all the right things,
but neglecting to mention
that a red thread on his hand
was tied to another.

But that's the thing about desperation,
it makes the weak sojourn
in the most dangerous territories.
And the worst thing is
he didn't need to labor
for my love.

I should've run away.
But I stayed, like a soldier's wife,
faithfully waiting for his return,
hoping he would
change his mind.

In the end, I was broken.
Not because he left,
but because he refused
to say goodbye.

The Red Thread

There was once a woman
who stayed in this room
where the air still held
the shape of his breath,
and the sheets remembered
how he whispered her name.

Around her wrist was a red thread
looped by a lover
who claimed her as his, forever.
Despite his sudden departure
and a promise never to return,
she remained in that room

She cried alone,
but held on to hope.
He would remember her.
So she wilted in the same bed,

a captive of her own aching faith,
waiting for his return.

Then the day came.
The door creaked open.
And there he was,
tall and familiar.
The red thread still wrapped
around his wrist.

She opened her arms,
ready to take him in,
until she saw the strangest thing.
There on his wrist
was another thread,
more vibrant than hers.

She kept her voice steady.
Kissed him once, softly,
Then cut the string swiftly.

She heard him calling her,

as she walked out the door.

But she never looked back.

Elle

I loved your name.
Hearing it made me feel
some type of way.
It rolled off my tongue
like silk and honey.
When I said it,
it felt like a kiss:
sweet nectarine, addictive.

Your name followed me everywhere:
on street signs,
the sides of cabs,
pages of books.
I became drunk on it,
obsessed with it,
sure I'd carry it forever.

I loved your name.

It belonged to me.

Or so I thought.

Now, I'm inconsolable

That I can't say it

without breaking my heart

into pieces,

because she's here.

And it's her

who will have your name.

Track No. 10

Do you remember the music
you shared with me?
You opened a world
I never thought to explore
had you not pointed to the door.

Suddenly, my playlist
was all about you,
each track a discovery
of pieces of you.

The swish of cymbals,
soft and shimmering, like your sighs.
The weep of saxophones,
as slow as your fingers.
The murmur of piano keys,
like your kisses on my skin.

I remember you on Sundays,
like clockwork.
And I wonder if,
somewhere between silence and static,
you think of me too.

If I could ask one thing of you,
let that one Amy song ring true,
and when it plays,
may you remember me too.

Drifted

Will you remember
that I used to walk through
these empty halls,
that I once enjoyed sustenance
from your unguarded breast,
taking as much as I could
without receiving a reprimand?

Would you let a piece of me
linger through the quiet rooms?
Will your children know
I once prayed to belong
under your eternal safekeeping?

But the truth is, I'm afraid
that no one will remember
that you used to be
the home of my hopes.
How could you ever let me go?

Why did you think

half a year is more than enough

to love me?

What did I do wrong?

Could I have done more?

Residues

Every night, I could only weep
For these feelings that I cannot use.
Every day, I'm obliged to bury
this love's residues.

It takes a space inside of me,
and there it sits in silence.
It feeds from me, and never leaves,
unmoved by all it's taken.

Its claws loosen in the morning.
An afterthought, a burning itch.
At night, it returns to steal away
my dignity.

I only ask you to depart
And free me from these feelings.

My dear, what good is my heart

If you don’t want it.

Pins and Needles

There was a blur of dark blues, maroons,
and blacks.
Busy tending the afflicted,
in Crocs and masks.

A young boy, maybe ten,
whimpered in the corner.
His face was wet with tears,
his left foot hovered over a box.

A woman in red satin sleepwear
casually walked by,
stood out among the masses.
And I stared at her, wondering
if she ran out of time.

The night felt like a lifetime.
And I sat there, all alone.
Nocturne creatures approached me,

alternating harvest.
Two took some blood.
Another listened to the beat of my heart.

I waited, half bored, half dreading the news,
until they returned to confirm
it wasn't anything
but my self-prescribed doom.
I was running out of fuel.
Got some dreams to catch on.
Got some thinking to do.

And I wonder if they knew,
the culprit was you.

Crack

I cannot name the feeling,
but it moves like a monster
coiling beneath my ribs.
As it grows, it tightens my breath,
squeezing my lungs.
A force so ruthless
it enfeebles my knees,
like rust corroding my sanity.
I sit through the hours
for that one greeting,
that single inquiry
that might break the silence.
But it never arrived.
And so I gnash my teeth
in self-loathing,
for letting the beast
breach my self-built prison.

How could he make me endure it?

How dare he

make me this vulnerable?

Spiral Folding

The room is dark.
Fan whirring as my insides
churn from hunger.
It's 3 o'clock.
My skin is damp,
suffering the summer.

The body obeys
the lively thoughts
that dangled in the shadows
of almost love,
or lack thereof,
as frightful as the scarecrows.

To bribe the gods
to make it so
or pull the roots this early.
I cannot feel

the way I did

that soured the previous summer.

If this is it,

be kind to me,

I cannot live forever.

Don't make it hard.

Don't feed the want.

Don't let it bloom through winter.

Bright Orange Coordinates

She was standing there motionless
in bright orange coordinates.
Bald and stiff, wearing white sneakers.
Skin as smooth as alabaster.

I sat there among the masses,
wondering if she'd like to run.
What lies beneath her sunglasses?
Why does she wear them without the sun?

Should I approach and steal away
her moment under the spotlight?
I looked at her, wanting to say,
"You could use a bit of sunlight."

But if I took her place instead,
would I get to win your sincerity?
Or should I just watch passing men
and further waste my dignity?

Or will I stand there motionless?

frozen, unable to run.

In bright orange coordinates.

In dark glasses, without the sun.

The Scourging of August

She used to meander in the dead of night,
hoping for an apparition
that would finally ease her heart.
In one of those nights,
she saw a phantom,
and like a hunter, she followed.
Her insides stirred, asking her to retreat,
and yet she kept her mission.

She sensed the time slowing down,
as her pulse started to race.
Before she could say a word,
the phantom turned,
revealing it was a stranger.

She kept her head low and walked away,
half disappointed, half relieved.

But then the next night,
and a couple of more,
she renewed her nightly duty.

This is how she squandered her time,
as callous as a child,
like she didn't suffer enough,
and didn't cry enough.
So she remained stuck in a loop
of torment.

But this was her reparation.
This was her cross to bear.
This was the price she paid,
for choosing them over herself.

In the Margins

I want you to know that
I never meant to drive
the stake into your heart.
But you should have known
the day would come
when I would no longer be able
to forge the strength to carry
your agonies.
Did you really believe
you could take from my vessel
without ever causing a drought?
If, as you said,
I didn't need to say that
the trees were green,
or that the seas were blue,
then why put me in a place
where I had to state the obvious?

Maybe I was meant to stab you
in the heart.
But you knew it was coming.
And quite frankly,
you deserved it.

Lucas

The pain you put on paper
for the demon you died for
outlived you in a world that you despised
and made a rich man
out of your tormentor.

Your written words gave him comfort,
but the guilty displayed no remorse,
and the world sat back, oblivious
of the price you paid for their joy.

The saddest thing was not your leaving,
it's the gold churned from your hurt.
The hearts of many you've easily won,
when all you wanted was the heart of one.

One of Your Girls

You wanted to kiss
the very thing
you were meant to leave behind;
as if it wouldn't protest,
as if it wouldn't break,
should you ever change your mind.
You thought you were free
to waste things
and never be
held accountable.
You didn't lie to her.
You lied to yourself.
You should've known,
you'd pay for her sorrow.

She only wished
she'd seen your true color
sooner.

Off the Meds

That space,
where the slightest shift
can send you falling,
and there's nothing
to break the fall.

That weight,
a heart beating off-key,
growing heavier by the minute,
tightening the breath,
summoning the tears.

That urge
to curl inward
and whimper through the night,
keeping the room in the dark.
So you can disappear.

That pain,
looming in the corner,
waiting for its turn
to unleash its rage
over the city.

Let it be felt today.
So tomorrow,
the veil can lift,
and then you can finally see
what your heart refuses.

This Is How I Loved You

I gave you time, not out of merit,
but only because you asked.
I let down my guard,
let you through the walls
that took me years to construct.
I risked my peace of mind,
sold my comforts,
so you can climb the ladder,
nailed by my desperation.

And there you were on my pedestal,
smug and grinning,
reciting lies, so natural,
they seemed unrehearsed,
so you can remain,
but still have the liberty
to leave as you pleased.
It was my throne

yet I was the one afraid
that you would let it go.

I deliberately dimmed my agency,
so you can shine brightly.
Yet, in the end, you have the audacity
to ask me what you did
despite seeing me
writhing under your feet.
So I've become unrecognizable:
an empty shell of a person
who crawled under her bed
etched horizontals on her pulse
scared the shit out of friends.

And so we came to this moment.
My long-awaited day of reckoning.
I hope the drink scalded you
and burned your conceit to the ground.
And if she had no doubts about you,

I hope the stain on your white shirt

did the job.

The Prelude Girl

The heat won't let her
escape into sleep.
Her hair's turning silver
from wounds buried deep.

She moves like the rest,
offering heart,
but seals it in glass
to keep it apart.

Each time she dared
to hand it whole,
they carved their names
and left a hole.

And so she has learned
to settle beneath
a surface of brave
but inside she bleeds.

And so every night
she's begging for sleep
but hard as she might
she never could sleep.

Sauver

At least concede
I was your favorite
out of all the mistakes
you've made.

May I haunt your sleep
like a siren
serenading you through your pain,
luring you back into sin.

I shall be your Roman Empire,
the what-the-fuck ending
of a film that endures
in your mind.

I'm not the one that got away,
I’m the one who must not be named.
Let the memory of my kisses
taste like blood in your mouth.

Go on and make me the villain—
twist your version to your liking,
fashion yourself as the martyr,
rewrite your guilt.

But I shall carry on
knitting regrets in your head,
so you can atone for all the sleep
you've taken.

Sandfly

I will retrace my steps
I shall dance and pray
For the innocence to return
But if I fail
I shall teach my body
To sway with the waves
And then on the sand
I will build my own castle
The one that bears my soul
So that you can never forget
My name.

Open Sea

You must learn to stand still in the presence of love,
to witness how it moves strangers,
mouths grazing in shadows,
fingers laced in quiet devotion,
the flushes on their cheeks,
eyes glinting with unspoken vows.

You may choose to avert your gaze
to be polite.
But ease your heart,
steady your breath,
like love is every day.
The way you wake up each morning,
and how the sun never misses a day.

Let love pass beside you,
like a river brushing the banks.
Do it until it stops being a stranger,

like it hasn't been away

for some time.

Until love remembers you.

Acknowledgment

My heartfelt gratitude to everyone who has inspired me to write this book.

To my family, my parents, Brenda and Hilario, and my siblings—Ate Ameriza, Vanessa Lorraine, Charnick Laus, Jake Naire, and Adriana Thalia—who are blissfully unaware that I am publishing this book, thank you for keeping me grounded. You are my inspiration, and even though we may not always verbalize our affections, please know that I will always love you.

To my friend Al Christopher Mendoza, who has shown unwavering support from day one, thank you so much. Your generosity knows no bounds, and your friendship is a true gift.

To my dear college friend Christine Moncada, though we may not see each other often, you remain one of my most cherished friends.

To my constants—Carlo Dominguez, Catherine Mendoza-Kaiser, Patria Marie Austria, Jonathan Espiña, Laarni De Lara, and Sunshine Morales—thank you for being my good friends and number one supporters.

Finally, thank you, Mike Alegado, for providing the captivating cover image for this book.

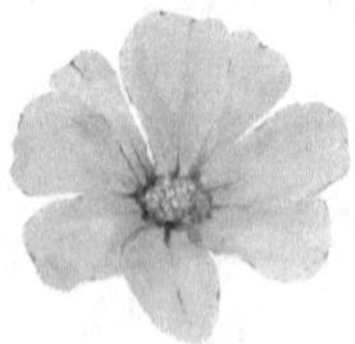

About the Author

MARJORIE GAVAN is a writer from Manila, Philippines, whose work explores heartbreak, identity, and quiet personal revolutions.

The Prelude Girl is her first poetry collection. She is also currently working on her debut novel.

www.ingramcontent.com/pod-product-compliance
Lightning Source LLC
LaVergne TN
LVHW090536110826
845146LV00003B/1128

* 9 7 9 8 9 9 1 8 6 7 9 2 4 *